Riverlight

for Annie

Theodore Deppe

RIVERLIGHT

ARLEN
HOUSE

Riverlight

is published in 2019 by
ARLEN HOUSE
42 Grange Abbey Road
Baldoyle
Dublin 13
Ireland
Phone: +353 86 8360236
Email: arlenhouse@gmail.com

978–1–85132–208–4, paperback

International distribution by
SYRACUSE UNIVERSITY PRESS
621 Skytop Road, Suite 110
Syracuse, New York
USA 13244–5290
Phone: 315–443–5534/Fax: 315–443–5545
Email: supress@syr.edu
www.syracuseuniversitypress.syr.edu

Typesetting by Arlen House

Cover Artwork: Caitlin Deppe

Contents

ACKNOWLEDGEMENTS

Thanks to the editors of *Crannóg, Cyphers, The North, The Onset Review* and *The Stinging Fly,* where some of these poems appeared, often in earlier versions.

Thanks also to Betsy Sholl, Caitlin Deppe, Kate Newmann and Joan Newmann who read these poems in early drafts and offered most helpful advice!

And thanks especially to Annie Deppe, first reader of each of these poems, and my heart's delight.

RIVERLIGHT

Cliffs of Fall

Fog and wet winds on the car ferry's deck
before we retreat inside. If we've seen

almost nothing, it hardly matters, the White Cliffs of Dover
are language first, Matthew Arnold and, older than that,

the last scenes of *King Lear,* and we are about to land
in the *Never, never, never, never, never*

of the broken king mourning Cordelia.
Another ferry passes through the mists like a ghost

and then a customs official welcomes us to England
asking, *What is the eventual doom*

of your car? I'm not sure I've heard correctly –
maybe he is joking – but he asks again, louder,

as if we don't understand English.
When we tell him our destination (*Yes, exactly, your doom*)

we are allowed into the country
of Keats and Virginia Woolf and Lewis Carroll.

A small road leads to the spectral cliffs
where we try out the officer's words,

asking each other, *What is your*
doom, tasting the strangeness of the mother tongue.

On Beauty

Our daughter joins us in Italy
with the perfect gift, a little time bomb
for the soul. Knowing how tight

the space in my carry-on bag is,
she's painted a one-by-two-inch portrait
of the most disruptive

of writers. The chaos I caused as a teenager
at a family dinner, bringing up Dostoyevsky:
God and the devil are at war over beauty

and the battlefield is the human heart.
Hard to say what lit that fire at our table.
Or why my mother left the room, weeping.

~

Across the Arno from our hotel,
a plaque marking the accommodations
where *The Idiot* was completed.

To avoid creditors back home, the honeymoon
with Anna lasted years, but Dostoyevsky
hated Florence's summer heat,

hated the autumn rains,
so Myshkin calls Italy *just a beautiful*
idea, a dream,

and any Russian journeying there
was indulging in *fantasy*.
Maybe Annie and Caitlin and I

are ready to live awhile in this dream of beauty –
things have been stressful
and a few happy days

sound heavenly – but what does Dostoyevsky
know about happiness?
Isn't he the patron saint

of laceration?
Of finding meaning
only through suffering?

Each night, I've unpacked the little portrait
and put it on my bedside table
and today I've placed it

on the dashboard, so Dostoyevsky
rides shotgun as we approach
the impossible town of Civita di Bagnoregio.

~

Pomegranates, that swing in the wind
between the open back door
and the garden

that's perched over the abyss
as sunlight turns the fruits' red skins
molten –

and the glowing quinces,
hanging like planets
above the Valley of the Badlands

where thin, bare, clay ridges
    stretch into the distance.
        When I first saw Civita, I thought

my fear of heights would keep me
    from climbing the steep footbridge
        to this pinnacle in the air,

but now I feel strangely at home
    in this improbable town that keeps losing
        medieval houses

as porous volcanic rock erodes
    and sends them plunging to the ravine. Opening
        a bottle of wine beneath the quince tree,

I find myself inside
    that oddly moving film, *Dream of Light,*
        a whole movie of Antonio López

painting the quince tree in his backyard
    and almost nothing happening – for two months,
        each morning, the artist stands

in the same spot, trying to catch the sunlight
    on those yellow fruits. Friends stop by
        to talk. The weather turns awful

and he raises a plastic canopy above the tree. Sirens
    wail. Somewhere off-screen bells ring.
        He works intently as the season passes

and the first fruits fall. Late November,
and a friend holds back a leaf with a rod
so López can sketch in a quince,

just as it was when he began. Beauty! His friend,
cold and tired of holding the rod, says, *This*
would be funny if it weren't so serious.

~

Dostoyevsky found beauty *unfathomable,*
found it *mysterious and terrible,*
eroding every stable place to stand.

And out of this mystery and terror he wrote his books.
During dinner in an Etruscan cavern
carved out of tufa rock,

our talk circles back to the meal my mother fled,
then to *The Brothers Karamazov*
which at fifteen I believed

an irrefutable argument for atheism.
Would the meal have gone better if I'd been
twenty-two and – having reread

the novel – proclaimed it a triumphant rebuttal
of the Grand Inquisitor? Or later, in my thirties,
when the book seemed an equal battle

between faith and doubt? An elderly woman brings
rounds of food almost too beautiful to eat:
candlelight flickers on zucchini pastries

and then little pockets of pasta appear,
nearly floating above their oval dishes,
and time seems to stop:

celebrations amid fire and shadows
in this wine cellar that is simultaneously
below the Alma Civita restaurant

and hundreds of feet above the valley.
It must be time to read *Karamazov* again.
Time to see just what sort of beauty

can truly satisfy.
Limoncello, and then our waitress
sings to herself as she climbs

the stairs to the kitchen, leaving us to the silence
of the cave, a quiet so sweet
that for a moment no one talks,

so we're astonished, emerging,
to find potted plants rolling downhill
as gales howl through Civita.

~

Come morning, though a few ripe fruits
have fallen from each tree,
the pomegranate and quince

I'd singled out in yesterday's photos
still shine in early sunlight.
The human heart as battlefield? *No, no,*

no, Mother would have said, *why think of Dostoyevsky*
in a moment like this? Can't you just enjoy
what's before your eyes?

Pomegranates that burn
with an intensity of their own. Quinces
that are a little knobby, a little

puckered, but gleaming like beaten gold.
And listen. If this is a combat zone,
why are you all so happy?

These fruits, in this unlikeliest of places.
And us. Mother, I lift my coffee mug
to the vista and salute you.

And then of course it is time to leave.
Annie and Cait walking in front of me
under a high Romanesque arch

that leads from the village
down into the spinning valley.
Beauty as portal.

Beauty as something to enter.
Then see what transpires
once we've dared let it inside.

Canzone Notturna

Learn Italian While You Sleep: hours
of hushed traveller's phrases

lulling the nightwalker into olive orchards
that lead down to sleep's sea

repeating, *Buona notte, buona notte.*
Let your breath becomes waves,

take the tender boat out to deep water
where the big dreams wait,

trust only in words, *viaggio dolce,*
and then something like *la bella*

confusione ...Your guide can take you only so far,
then you're on your own.

The day before my walk began, I decided not to take my camera, forcing myself to observe things closely, find words to describe them. An adolescent's mistake! I would love to have a photographic record of those narrow roads and long-ago faces, and my journals, so head-in-the-clouds, are barely usable. What had I expected, starting with *The Divine Comedy* and continuing with a list of philosophers and theologians and Keats, Wordsworth, Yeats and Dylan Thomas? And, I was nineteen.

~

March 1970, the beginning of a six-month
        independent study, and I fell in love
                with sleeping on the ground

(the earth more supple
        than expected). I was walking to Assisi,
                imagining I could learn Italian

from a dual-language Dante,
        reading of the four great rivers of hell
                while I sat beside the Arno,

plum trees clouding the hills,
        and one night I slept in an olive grove,
                my back to the warm stone wall

and dreamt of a woman
        who had become my guide.
                Even when I woke

she was there: the wind
        passed through the orchard and olive leaves
                kept changing from silver to green.

Bread and pecorino cheese for breakfast
and I wrote my sister,
asking her to find a particular sentence

in *The Dharma Bums.*
Two weeks later, I read,
The closer you get to real matter,

rock air fire wood, boy, the more spiritual
the world is.
Cross-country hitchhiking

got me through the high school years,
but going for a long walk
was different –

rock air fire wood.
Someone was leading me
but she wouldn't say where.

~

1970. When eighteen and nineteen-year-olds were still being sent to kill or be killed in Vietnam. On the train from Italy to Ireland, I read a Chekhov story, 'Gooseberries', in which happiness is considered a disaster if one forgets about the sufferings of others.

~

April, the first night in Ireland.
Camped outside Wexford, I started
Bonhoeffer's *Letters and Papers from Prison.*

He wrote, *It is possible to get used*
to physical hardships
and to live for months

out of the body, so to speak,
and I wondered if his book
was wrong for this hike? I wanted to be in

my body as much as possible.
But, since jail for draft resistance
was a possibility when I returned

to the States, I tried to envision him
in Cell 92 of Tegel Prison.
The bucket. The stench.

As Bonhoeffer wrote his parents,
To picture a cell does not need
much imagination – the less you use,

the nearer the mark you will be.
Just details, then. Physical things:
in that manmade, concrete world,

a small round stone in the courtyard;
air's movement on a warm May evening;
not fire bombs (though what else

can one think of as those incendiary
explosives shake the night?) –
the certainty

of morning sun; and the wood-plank bed
beneath the open
barred window.

Oh, and all those miles:
eighteen months of walking
three hours a day in a seven-by-ten-foot cell:

three steps and a pivot.
Those hikes he made
in the Harz Mountains when he

was nineteen. Three steps
and a pivot.
Because of Bonhoeffer

and against the backdrop
of the Vietnam War,
I read daily from a psalter,

that compendium of faith and doubt.
Bombs fell at night, deepening
his knowledge of the psalms

and then, after the all-clear, he listened
to see if the thrush in the prison yard
had any songs left.

The last thing he wanted to do
was start a letter to his parents
and tell them

how thankful he was.
The bird didn't feel like singing.
So, Bonhoeffer began,

writing in its silence.
There was nothing much to say.
The cell was chilly,

his head
ached from lack of sleep.
Still, one might make a psalm of it.

~

Moon Reflecting Fire. All these years later, I'm rereading my friend Doug Anderson's poems about his tour in Vietnam. I might have ended up in those jungles, looking for tripwires among the underbrush instead of visions of Beatrice. Doug, interrogating that other life, writes, *Our bones knew what we'd done.*

~

Horizontal rain outside a pub in Waterford
where I drank tea,
writing my parents

after harrowing news stories
of carpet bombing in Laos and Cambodia.
Then I moved on

to my assigned lesson,
accompanying nineteen-year-old Wordsworth
to revolutionary France.

Bliss was it in that dawn to be alive,
But to be young was very heaven.
Reading *The Prelude,*

I wondered if I should be back in the States,
marching with others
instead of walking alone.

For so many in those years, being young
was a transmutation of hell's flames.
Soon enough, I'd rejoin

the antiwar protests in Washington,
but for now *The lonely roads were schools to me,*
and *rock air fire wood* remained my mantra,

which was when the black-haired waitress,
Sinéad, began singing along
as the radio played the new Beatles tune.

Strange pilgrim. The woman I'd cared so much about
had entered a convent and the woman
I would come to love and marry

was in the future,
so in adolescent confusion I carried
the new song to Carrick-on-Suir

and beyond. Call it the via negativa.
... Nah nah nah nah, Hey Jude!
A day later, in the shelter I'd found

beneath rhododendrons,
I made a sketch of black clouds
above my little cell,

then closed the notebook
when the first drops spotted the page.
Beyond me, the River Suir,

gloriously stippled with rain,
while I sat out the shower
like a child watching a pageant

of cloudburst and flow.
        When the squall passed,
                I was loath to leave my bower (just once,

surely, bower is the right word?)
        so, as I lingered,
                it was there I heard the sound

of wings on water as two swans clambered
        into the air and flapped past me,
                over the glancing river that seemed

at once an elemental highway
        and a state of mind, so I was sure I was in
                one of Wordsworth's *spots of time,*

though not the sort you return to later,
        for nourishment and delight – this was right
                now.

~

Right now. Almost fifty years ago. As in, *Now as I was young and easy* ... In the fullness of that moment, beneath those illuminated leaves, there were still four months to walk and parcels of books that would arrive like celebrations, c/o Poste Restante, in a sequence of towns that circled Ireland.

And once below a time I woke to find the rain had cleared and dizzy stars blazed above the River Suir. The wisdom of the dream I'd just climbed out of delighted me: the inner life and outer life might be the same. Which didn't make sense in the morning. Until I started walking.

In a Chinese Landscape

For Annie, on hearing that Washington's Freer Gallery is closed for renovation

When they've finished remodelling, will it still be possible for dry leaves to enter when a door opens, will they still be able to gust down long galleries and surprise a pair of museum goers who have immersed themselves right to left in a Chinese landscape's folding screen? Forty-something years ago that couple was us, following the mist-filled, not-quite-of-this-world valleys into the vertical peaks of mountains that dragonflyed up through clouds. A bridge over a torrent. A pine tree on a bare ridge. And a single traveller who pauses for a moment to watch dazzling water rush past and centuries later still lingers. So often in Sung landscapes or T'ang poetry there's just the one wanderer, and the year before we visited the Freer I'd walked a thousand-mile circle around Ireland, revelling in solitude. Was walking so long by myself somehow necessary? Arriving home, thinned by the roads and a little wild, when else could I have caught the eye of one so lovely? On that trip to Washington we got so lost in Chinese mountains that the autumn leaves, approaching on the wings of spring wind, startled us, arriving like messengers from some other world.

Inauguration Night

Because last week I read how a clerk
in Dostoyevsky's *The Idiot* tried to comfort

Nastasya by reading to her from the *Book of Revelations*
and because today three different friends joked

about the Apocalypse arriving now,
I turn to John of Patmos to see what hope he offers.

One can only watch so much news
from Washington without risking despair,

but the Gospels offer solace, it seems,
though first the sun over Seattle

will turn black as sackcloth, the moon over Milwaukee
blood red, and stars will fall on Sarasota

while the people of Pittsburgh retreat to caves
and the pale rider devastates the Bible Belt.

Back for a last check on the news – no sign
yet of the Great Dragon appearing on Trump Tower –

and then I read before bed, Dostoyevsky again,
where by dreamlike chance I find a consumptive boy

quoting an Angel from the Apocalypse:
And there shall be no more time.

He means that time will end for him when he dies
though I wonder if the Bible means life itself

will slam shut. Night falls on America, I try to sleep,
then search for the earlier passage in which Myshkin

meditated on those same words
and found a different meaning: *There shall be*

no more time describes that last second
before a seizure strikes,

when everything is beautiful and unified,
when one might visit in an instant

the many rooms of paradise.
Myshkin describes a moment so blessed

that he would trade his whole life if he had to.
I get up and – forgive me – check the news,

then step outside to see if the constellations are holding
tight, and the bells from the harbour and blurry stars

feel part of a dream that can't be explained
but that knows and means more than is apparent.

Later, the wind has a lot to say on this first night
of the next four years. I can't remember who said

Despair is the one sin that can't be forgiven,
but Prince Myshkin said, *Beauty shall save the world.*

Morning brings news of millions of women
marching in Washington and around the country,

around the planet, a heartening swell of resistance.
And these words scribbled on the paper by my bedside table:

There shall be no more time for keeping silence.
Or there shall be no more time.

On the Music of the Naughtingels

A middle-of-the-night letter to Kate and Joan Newmann

We hear you're off to Crete!
It's ten years since Annie and I
travelled there with you,

and I keep coming back to the little house
where El Greco might have been born. It was
closed, so the *Lonely Planet* guide to Crete

might be excused for not mentioning
its existence. But outside its locked doors
we heard the sweetest birdsong –

blackbird or thrush, probably not
a nightingale, though once I raised that possibility
Joan recited Keats' ode

and the light under that carob tree seemed to flicker in
dactyls and iambics, like a conversation
between the living and the dead.

On Keats' birthday, Annie and I visited
the Hampstead house where the ode
was composed. And recalling Joan's recital,

I decided to memorise the poem,
to find a home for it in my heart –
so I started at the beginning,

My heart aches, and a drowsy numbness pains
My sense, as though of hemlock I had drunk –
Oh, I wish I'd begun when I was younger,

when it was easier to recall things,
          yet even the attempt keeps opening up
                    some shared life. One of the two of you

recommended we read Patrick Leigh Fermor,
          and I loved his account
                    of capturing a Nazi general

and leading him into the mountains of Crete.
          The prisoner, gazing at snow-covered Mount Ida,
                    quoted in Latin about a mountain

shining in a winter storm, and Fermor continued
          the ode by Horace where the general left off,
                    so they traded stanzas known by heart

and, Fermor wrote, *things were different between us*
          for the rest of our time together.
                    In *A Time of Gifts,*

Fermor writes that each try at boarding school
          had proved *a uniform disaster,*
                    so he embarked on a walk

across Europe, all the way
          to Constantinople. I enjoy his
                    descriptions of birdlife –

the line of storks that stretched
          across the sky in Hungary,
                    or the morning he woke to see two hoopoes

which, when they took to the air,
          turned into little flying zebras!
                    And there were nightingales,

which led him not only to recite Keats from memory
but to transpose the ode backward,
first words, then phrases, then sentences,

until, spoken fast enough, it sounded like an unknown
language. *Away, away, for I will fly to thee*
became *Yawa, yawa, rof I lliw ylf ot eeht!*

Oh, there's so much to tell you, so much to ask.
Reading *Finnegans Wake* last night, I came upon
an enchanted passage about *the naughtingels*

and when I put down the book, I courted sleep
by repeating words from my reading, *nocturnefield,*
lightandgayle, waldalure, naughtingels,

until I almost heard them singing in a dream.
But, just before sleep, I realised
that *naughtingels* might also be not-angels

and I confess I broke my rule
and turned on the Internet at night
to make sure we were still here

as our so-called leaders have threatened each other
with nuclear war.
Already with thee! tender is the night –

After months of caring for his dying brother,
naugtingels might have been for Keats
angels of nothingness.

Ten years ago, dining by a shining river
on our way back to Nikos Kazantzakis Airport,
we heard a bird in a high cage –

Annie thought it might
be a nightingale. If so,
I hope when autumn came

it didn't dash itself to death
as some imprisoned singers do,
flinging itself against the bars,

trying to follow its migratory impulse to Africa.
Africa – what a joy it was
staying together

on the south coast of Crete,
gazing out over the Libyan Sea,
so many colours of blue.

Well, safe travels and much love.
I'll close my eyes soon and listen
to Joan recite, *Away! Away!*

and Paddy Fermor respond *Yawa! Yawa!*
and James Joyce up the ante with
the dewfolded song of the naughtingels.

I have not finished getting the poem by heart yet,
but some night, if the planet makes it that long,
I'll be able to ask

Was it a vision, or a waking dream?
Fled is that music. Do I wake or sleep?
(Od I ekaw ro peels?)

Kreuzberg Sonata

Tell me about a time when we were happy –

Between the apparition of the six-storey businessman
and the night his mural was blacked out
there were a few years when almost everything flourished –

Tell me about the time when there was less worry –

Between the businessman's appearance, covering
a housing block's windowless side wall,
and the night the painter took it back, protesting
landlords who raised rents because of chic street art,
there were autumns when we sublet a flat from friends
and I wrote heartfelt letters to students,
some of whose names I've already forgotten,
then stepped out with you each day
into the city of second chances.

Tell me about time –

I'm circling back to Wordsworth, who said there are
spots of time – moments past
that still feed and heal us –
but I say there were whole seasons
when Kreuzberg gave us room to explore,
street by street, the possibilities of joy.
On each of the businessman's hands
a gold watch doubled as a handcuff,
connected as they were by a gold chain,
but we thought time was a place we could walk through,
we'd cross the Oberbaumbrücke
and riverlight blazed in your hair.

Oh, once inside a time of two gold watches
in an April of still-folded buds, the sun moved
so slowly above the waters that the moment almost lasted.

~

At the Café Edelweiss, on our way home
from hearing Beethoven's *Kreuzer Sonata,*
we ordered our first martinis ever –

Can you make us ones like in the movies, please?
Two French girls entered
and, hearing the recording of Edith Piaf,

sang along, *Je vois la vie en rose,*
and when the next verse began
the German couple sitting near us

joined in, in French, and their dog –
it must have been part greyhound – looked up
at all the singing, then caught my gaze

and turned away.
I'd like to think he was as happy as the rest of us
and was just shy

but maybe it suffered *Weltschmertz,* or *Lebensmüde,*
maybe the song it wanted to sing was
Oh you don't know the shape I'm in.

~

I woke to hard rain on Falckensteinstraße
and wrote down the fragment of a dream.
In the Kentucky hospital where I once worked
a woman begged to use the nursing station telephone:
Doesn't everyone get to make one last call?

Her husband reassured her, *We're all here, Darling,*
you don't need to call anyone,
but he hadn't understood,
she didn't want to call home, she needed
to call the bus company that has the lioness on the side

and did I have the number? And no, it wasn't Greyhound.
Any child on the street would know the lioness
that passes all understanding. I woke in the grey hour and
wished I'd long ago found and memorised the number
of the lioness, for just such a night, just such a traveller.

~

And once, in this city with few strays, a dog
hopped on the train at Warschauer Straße
and beamed at those of us who paid

for our tickets, on its way perhaps to a friendly grocer,
or ready for the streets' maze, and I thought it a kindred
spirit of the boy I'd convinced myself I once was, free

to explore my hometown, go anywhere I liked, on foot
or by bike, no-handed, maybe eyes closed for a while,
giving myself to the summer's breeze.

We called it the Black Dog of Happiness
and looked for it each time we boarded the U-Bahn,
though it never reappeared.

But two years later, we were surprised
by an arthritic dog easing over the gap to the train.
It let its lame legs buckle

so it could tuck under an empty seat
and regard us from safety. It was smaller than Happiness,
who in any case couldn't have grown that old so quickly,

but it met my eyes and studied me.
I fear he found me wanting.
Maybe he was the Greying Dog of Philosophy

and he took the train to the end of the line,
to Uhlandstraße, then roused himself
to climb the stairs with the rest of us,

walking into the light of a Berlin morning. Why can't
Philosophy and Happiness be the same dog?
We tried to walk with him awhile,

then did our best to keep him in sight,
but hobbled as he was he had four legs
and went somewhere we could not follow.

~

No, no, tell me about the time when we were happy,
when there was music almost every day –

Oh, once in a café we heard a radiantly-young octogenarian
from Jena. Her accordion,

weathered by sun and the black rain of decades,
was some sort of time machine.

One jig transported us all back to a year when she busked
in Ireland and the night in County Clare

when she heard the great Joe Cooley play, a gig arranged
when Cooley was dying

though there was joy in the cross-talk of musicians, joy
in the pulsing noise

and faces of family and friends who crowded around
the winter's session.

And her next tune was a waltz she wrote in Warsaw,
insouciant triple time

leading to a café near the Jewish theatre where a novelist
was waiting, a man she knew she shouldn't

meet, but did, and she wasn't sure whether to call
her waltz 'A Critique of Pure Reason'

or 'All the Merry Things That Shouldn't Have Happened',
but it's a song that slips past

rules and miles and years. She kept trying not to smile,
but her eyes shone.

You ask about happiness and I think of what we learned
from her that night.

Work the bellows like a gale. Play the buttons
like soft rain.

Style

Youth and mirth and carelessness
        flicked a still-burning butt
                through the window of a parked Mercedes,

and the car was locked, of course, the window's opening
        too narrow to retrieve the cigarette
                which would not go out,

so she high-heeled inside for a pitcher
        and then, as traffic passed, stood as inconspicuously
                as a six-foot blonde in vintage black could,

sloshing ice water onto the sheepskin seat.
        She admitted later that it was Man Ray's short film
                of Picasso smoking

that she'd been imitating: in a silly wig,
        playing the part of Carmen, Picasso
                repeatedly failed to strike a match,

then lit the cigarette with great flair and
        beamed as he flamencoed the match away.
                Hoping the car's owners wouldn't return

to an inexplicable pillar of fire, she brought a second pitcher
        and then it was time to leave, quickly
                but with no hint of hurry,

twisting her hair into a simple flame
        and striding off down the centre
                of the suddenly combustible street.

READING THE *WAKE* IN BROAD DAYLIGHT

In the name of Annah the Allmaziful, the Everliving, the bringer of Plurabilities, haloed be her eve, her singing sung, her rill be run, unhemmed as it is uneven!

– James Joyce, *Finnegans Wake*

Rain on Galway's windows. Hoping not to disturb
Annie's sleep before her cataract surgery, I'm camped out

in our B&B's bathroom, reading *Finnegans Wake:*
Words weigh no more to him than raindrips to Rethfernhim.

Which we all like. Rain. When we sleep. Drops.
Though I'm far from being Joyce's ideal reader, I do

suffer the insomnia that he recommends and many nights
I turn to his *book of the dark* to let its dream logic

lure me back to the realms of sleep. So much to worry about,
but for now I follow the *meandertale,* letting myself become

A Wondering Wreck, passing between *Skilly and Carubdish,*
pleased to contemplate the *orangotangos* –

~

From the bedroom, I seem to hear Annie singing
in her sleep, a low, amused tune, as if Lauren Bacall

had set a speech of Anna Livia Plurabelle to music,
and I open the bathroom door a crack to listen.

Annie's gentle breathing. Only that. But, *joygrantit,* that.
I climb back into bed, dressed now in my *mirthday suit,*

letting myself move through that maze of puns,
halfway *between Druidia and the Deepsleep Sea.*

~

Usually I only read the *Wake* at night, but how could I not
bring it to the waiting room, a place that feels dreamlike

enough with its own subliminal fear. Joyce called his left eye
the broken window of my soul, and the many surgeries

he suffered for it meant he worked on his last book
squinting out through shivers of light

at notecards and crayons. Nora asked what he was doing
with all those cards and he said, *Trying to write a masterpiece.*

~

I'm just reading and scribbling words in my notebook
till my wife appears in the doors leading from surgery

and I can say, *Hiphip champouree! Anneliuia!*
What was the song I thought I heard her singing in her sleep?

Was the rain speaking through her lips? Annie's surgery
is taking longer than I expected. Strange comforter, Joyce,

whose phobias included thunder, firearms, dogs and water.
This is not the time to think about the descriptions

I've read of Joyce's operations, or to think too much
about Stephen Dedalus being threatened, *Apologise, apologise*

or *the eagles will come and pull out his eyes.*
Go back towards the beginning, a little past *riverrun,*

find *Arrah, sure, we all love little Anny Ruiny,*
or, we mean to say, lovelittle Anna Rayiny,

when unda her brella, mid piddle mid puddle
she ninnygoes nannygoes nancing by. Yoh!

~

No news yet, and an Englishman who likes to talk
has taken the seat next to me, and when he ignores the fact

I'm reading and writing and keeps talking,
I let myself ask odd questions, including, *People talk*

in their sleep, but is it possible to sing in your sleep? And
doesn't he have a daughter who has sung from her dreams

since she was an infant? *She's sixteen now,* he says,
and won't her future partner be surprised,

but really, isn't it wonderful, that something in her
needs, most nights, to come out in song?

~

This time when the door opens
it's Annie. I hold her, saving the greeting

I'd copied from the *Wake* for later: *Vivi vienne, little*
Annchen! Vielo Anna, high life! Sing us a sula, O, susuria!

Path to the Water

Removing the wind rock, unfastening the latch, I pass
through the wooden gate

and follow the lane that becomes a mown path skirting
the lavender-coloured potato fields

that slope down to the North Atlantic. No one else awake
except the blackbird and its song.

This same path has appeared in different times and places,
in Wales, once, and on Cape Cod

and that mist-filled dawn near Lissadell. Always the same
blue gate, the same slope, this dreamlike

feel in the waking day, like sleepwalking to the sea.
I have been here before.

Each time, it's a kind of death, that can't be helped.
Then walking back home to you, restored.

To you. As long as that is possible. As long as the sea is blue
and there are gates. And paths that lead both ways.

Summer, Renvyle

Summer in Ireland can be a question
of moments. This year
it arrived as I walked home

from my morning swim,
yellow irises offering their jolts
of colour to the meadow

and two hares dashing off
through waving grasses,
only the tips of their ears visible.

GALWAY

Of the portrait of an old man in the breakfast room,
a saint or beggar, I'm told, *Oh, he's*
nobody. What is it about this rough portrait –

the flowing beard, the partly balding head, the sad
kind eyes – that made me ask our hostess about it?
She bought it for five euros from a German doctor

on Henry Street – a little bit of the big world brought
to Nun's Island. A derelect or holy man or both.
After breakfast, a walk along the River Corrib and I gaze

at the harbour from a bench dedicated
to *Dr Joe MacHale, 1901–1977, the kindest man in town.*
All morning I inquire about this man of exceptional

kindness, but no one seems to know who he was.
There was an archbishop in Tuam named MacHale,
that's probably your man. Or maybe he was

a harbourmaster, or else the rugby great, *the gallant*
little Blackrock College boy, Joe McHale? You can be so beloved
that a bench recalls you in the harbour's heart

and four decades later you're one more nobody.
And the painter who signed his name so modestly
that it's illegible? And the man who posed for him?

In Charlie Byrne's Bookshop a cover photo shows
a man with just such a white beard, Victor Hugo, a writer
who urged the practice of small kindnesses.

This evening, online, I find a Dr Joe McHale, 1900–1977,
and though spelling and dates differ slightly,
I think my search is done. If so, he interrupted

his medical studies after the Easter Rising
to join the IRA, then was jailed in Galway, where his
sixteen-year-old friend and cellmate was put to death.

And in 1940, he was called at night to a district court,
where a domestic servant was arraigned.
A guard showed Dr McHale a suitcase

containing a full-term female infant.
Was a man of kindness ever needed more?
The servant girl from the Midlands had been alone

near the pier when she was stopped,
but the doctor said the child was stillborn,
there were no signs of violence,

this was a time for mercy.
I've found her name at last, Maire Ní Colgain,
but after she returned home

no further word. I hope she wasn't one more Irish woman
disappeared in the Magdalenes.
The court records in Galway say

a friend paid her way home, writing her parents
to say she'd been ill. This was 1940, a few months
after the Nazis invaded Poland

and maybe the same night
Louis MacNeice paced this grassy pier,
writing his poem, 'Galway'

(A hundred swans /dreaming on the harbour,/
The war came down on us here).
The Corrib flows past a bench with the name

of a man who seems mostly forgotten. The shining
          river rushes past, erasing our signatures.
Dr Joe McHale, or MacHale, whoever you were

          I'm grateful for whatever kindness
you showed a young woman
          who was not after all nobody, at least to you.

On Not Seeing Mweelrea

Wet sands add to the dazzle –
a morning so bright

the mountains in the east

disappear and the shouts
and laughter of children

racing across the blind beach

are the sort of gold
one might indeed

take into the next world.

The White Strand
of Renvyle

at the foot of this August day.

First, the woman left, then swallows appeared in the back garden's fog, dozens of them between the mist-grey car and his neighbour's grey-green trees – as if, in the man's sorrow, it was still permitted to look from his window and be visited by wonder. And all morning they were there, darting and weaving above this one charmed corner of the world, skimming tall grasses. She had lingered, unsure, all summer, not wanting to be like Paolo and Francesca, deeply in love but doomed to circle hell. When he stepped outside, his presence didn't matter, the swallows flashed past and turned bat-quick, harvesting the air in elaborate figure eights. To them, was he there and not there? Then, after lunch, they were gone, the migration had begun. She had told him, *If I ever get a tattoo it will be a swallow like sailors wear, since they know how to find their way home.* There is some art that watches birds, but it's not his. She's out there, travelling, somewhere, and he's watching the empty space in the back garden between his car and his neighbour's grey trees. No, not grey, almost nothing is ever just grey she told him, it's mulberry or plum-grey, more than just one thing. Before migration was understood, swallows were said to hibernate in pond bottoms or winter on the moon. The man thinks they're not much better understood these days. The middle of September: is that when it happens? *Season of mists* and all good wishes. The flocks could be flying over Gibraltar or crossing the Sahara, pushing on to South Africa, and the woman must be travelling even farther – is that possible? – heading home, wherever that happens to be, under autumn skies.

On Friendship

Mirage that makes the seven-mile causeway
to Antelope Island
look impassable.
Then a tablecloth

spread on a hill
while below us a buffalo herd
wanders past. Oh, miracle Brunello

and spanakopita picnic for four. Across the lake,
snow squalls move along the Wasatch range,
but on the island,
warm March sunlight
and the stories of friends. Emily's visit to her family

on spring break, and the invitation
to her mother's women's group.
All the problems of the world solved
over a pot of tea. Eighty,
ninety years old, so the problem was usually

death. One woman, who died
in the hospital parking lot and was *resurrected*,
told the group, *It's easy*
to die. You don't even notice it.

Second round of wine. Red-winged blackbirds,
pronghorn antelope, and when I sneak off
to piss, a buffalo that lets me know I'm getting
too close.

Later, when Tomas asks about our spring break,
there's dodging Indiana's deadly volley of tornadoes
and the airport shuttle driver's bravado:
The boss said, if I see a twister, just floor it!

And how, nearing Indianapolis, the skies
I'd been scanning simply filled in.
We learned later a funnel cloud
formed behind that screen
but did not step through. A supercell clothed in rain,
in fog, in hail. And the storm
slowed traffic so much, we couldn't have fled
even if we had seen the devil.

The strange part was, all afternoon this talk of death
in the best of spirits.
Emily says, *Gee, this is like*
going to a party with Ingmar Bergman.
And Annie, *I think I would have liked that.*

The problem of death. Is it, then, a spectacular
nothing? Grey – a sort of red-blue-grey – no edge,
but thunder sounding within, and lightning
that is the stuff of dreams.

It's easy to die. And wine that tastes this good.
Enough. We've just heard
what I'm told is a western meadowlark,

a fanfare
so clear and loud it seems right next to us.
Then one sees the singer
down the road on a post.
The bird's head lifted.
The song all around us.

View from the Roof

Gladly, I would have refused this chance
to join my wife and eldest son on the garage roof!

Three-hour's drive home through squalling snow
and I was greeted not with a hot bath, whiskey

and early bed, but by calls to climb the borrowed ladder
and help shovel out. The storm had stopped,

I suggested this could wait till morning, but an hour ago
wet snow stove in the neighbour's carport.

Now, from the roof, we watch night clouds
sweep over the Holyoke range: I didn't know

you could see those hills from our home.
Up and down the block, a necklace of brilliantly lit

back rooms facing the bike path, as if neighbours
I've rarely or never met each want to invite travellers in

for wine and talk. Lopsided moon
and a few bright stars between the ridge and clouds –

how many gifts like this have I returned unopened?

RAIN STICK

Four-year-old Alanna lifts the rain stick
and pebbles or beans
or whatever is in there tumbles down

the hollow tube of dried cactus making a sound
like the middle of those wet nights
we miss in Ireland

when everything starts staccato
then surges and cascades,
an elemental celebration.

Seamus Heaney's rain stick poem
comes to mind, the one
where heaven might be entered

not through the eye of a needle but
Through the ear of a raindrop.
My father died the same summer

as Heaney, the same year
Alanna was born,
and when she turns the stick

upside down again
the music arrives as bidden, mixed tones
that rattle and plunge and come

feelingly undone, a water-horde
descending from what had seemed to be
clear sky.

Approaching the Far-Off Palace of Solomon

Busking is for the young, but this woman
with long grey braids plays *The Arrival*
of the Queen of Sheba on tenor sax
as we wait for the MTA at Porter Square

and I remember Robert J. Lurtsema
starting Morning Pro Musica
with bird song, then letting those calls
mingle with this pageantry from Handel.

She plays on as I board the train
and I recall those years when I worked weekends
and how any Sunday off meant I was in my wife's
world, which always included *the Queen of Sheba.*

After that fanfare-turned-sinfonia,
Robert J. took *a look at some of the items in the news*
and read the terrible bulletins in an impossibly low, calm,
almost comforting voice, speaking slowly, stopping

as if to think, long pauses with no dead air time
as he seemed to be trying to fathom Iran-Contra,
the Challenger explosion, Chernobyl, or whatever disaster
we'd brought upon ourselves that week.

Then, music and leisurely talk or play,
followed by my wife's dream of breakfast.
Sunday's playlist always wheeled around a Bach cantata
and I knew Annie would have liked best to be on stage again

watching for the conductor's turn towards the altos.
Anywhere she was in the house
she'd be ready to join in, and sometimes the children and I
stopped what we were doing and listened as Annie

merged with the music and something wild and visionary
roamed the kitchen, swirled through the bedrooms and
hallways, claimed its space in the room of the living.
This afternoon, jotting down these notes

as the Red Line jostles me along,
I'm grateful for those moments when our home
became a place where music triumphed over headlines
and a young mother took her part in the chorus.

A Short History of Sleep

Don't play what's there. Play what's not there
– Miles Davis

Just before sleep, a call
about our grandson's high fever:
though our son's car is in the shop,

he thinks there's no need yet
for us to drive over, but still, could we
for once keep our phone by the bed?

For a long while, I try to cross
the blurred boundary into dreams
with one ear in the pillow, one

alert for a ring tone, telling myself that
ever since our ancestors stopped
sleeping in trees, we've been doing just that,

relaxing into a vigilance that lets us rest
while knowing death might seek us
with the softest feet we don't hear.

Decades ago, I slept in the only
empty bed in a psychiatric hospital.
I'd worked evening shift, they needed

help on days, and since home
was in the next state, I hoped
the room wouldn't be needed

for a new admission. I learned
what all the patients knew – someone
might wander in at any time –

but I was exhausted, and I'd just read
about the woman who gave up
name and history to become Peace Pilgrim.

At the end of her first
cross-country walk, she slept
in Grand Central Station, then woke

with the radiant impression
that a celestial orchestra played
during the night and she could

still hear echoes. If she could sleep
in that hub of transience and power,
I could give myself to the tentative

silence of hospital dark.
Eventually, my journal records, I did,
but first I spent an hour

roughing out a short story
about a man who might have slept
in that bed the night before.

I made him a gentle, bipolar
Chinese-American jazz musician
who briefly played with Miles Davis.

My sax player (I called him Terrance Cheng)
would have been in trouble, that's why
he was in the hospital, that's why there might

be a story worth writing about him.
Say he'd been awake two straight days,
and he knew what lack of sleep could do.

Before dropping out of university,
he'd crammed for a Shakespeare final,
staying up the way I once did, reading

every assigned play. Midway
through the exam he lost track of his logic,
returned to the start of his sentence

but couldn't make the words out,
then couldn't even get the letters
to cohere to form words.

No further news from the burdened
and beloved household
of our single-parent son –

maybe they're all sleeping.
Is that what life comes down to,
finding a way to rest

surrounded by trouble?
I say some of the old prayers
for our children and grandchildren

then lie down and picture Terrance Cheng
released from the hospital
and reunited with his saxophone

before leaving his halfway house.
Does he try out a little Dexter Gordon,
then a Shostakovich prelude?

I have him make up a song he calls
The Kingdom of Everyone is Safe.
Like Miles in his mellowest mood,

playing music that might calm us.
Playing notes that couldn't
possibly be there. I wish I could imagine

what that would sound like –
maybe something to do with Miles
telling his musicians not to play the idea

that's there but instead to play the next one.
Dreams might understand that,
but since I can't sleep yet

I turn the thought upside down, imagine my musician
on the road, learning to play
what is. Like Peace Pilgrim, who slept under bridges,

or on the concrete floor of gas stations,
in haystacks or cemeteries
(quiet places where the grass

is usually neatly trimmed),
he would need to find places to rest,
so tonight I picture him

stretching out like her
in Manhattan's great concourse.
After decades of learning to play

what's not there, he pays attention
to the soft static of the loudspeaker
as it blurs a destination, *Schenectady*,

and the sound of a fretful child
during the endless wait (may Emrys and Alanna
be fast asleep now, and Michael, and me, too, soon).

Above him, the station's great arches and windows,
and then the gold-leaf constellations
on the ceiling. Echoes of the other world.

I let him name the clusters of the almost
everlasting stars and make a sort of music
of the list: Ursa Major, Pegasus, Ursa Minor, Orion.

Maybe that's when it comes to him,
a fragment of the melody Peace Pilgrim
heard, that radiant song of *what is,*

the music inside everything.
Listen, Terrance Cheng tells me through the threshold
of a dream. *Listen, deeper.*

Your lullaby begins,
'Now I lay us down to sleep
in the Grand Central of All Travellers …'

VOYAGERS

Rather than peer through blurred lenses,
I tuck my glasses into the raincoat's pocket
and the drops on my hood sound like the play

of rain on a tent when it's possible to sleep late.
Bass notes of surf below as I climb the headland

and the sprung rhythm of bell buoys,
mad with spondees. From those buoys, sea lions call,
and from ferns, glistening near the abyss,

the song of a wren. I watch the crumpled Pacific, hoping
for a glimpse of grey whales heading north,

but if they are out there they pass unseen,
letting fog horns take their place. I try to respond
by imitating Mongolian throat singing, rolling

a low Oooooo-sound around my tongue,
but can't find that harmonic overtone

that the writer Dermot Healy once tried to teach me
in a pub in Letterkenny, a sound as much prayer
as growl though his gift frightened some patrons.

Years later, his body was removed from the wake house
in Maugherow to a farewell of throat music.

I go down into my chest and am trying to send
paired tones out across the water when a hiker
with unruly hair rounds the path and catches me

mid-song. Rather than avert his eyes or laugh
he beams at me, roars, *Good man!*

then lumbers off. O brother,
could that have been you? What distances
did you travel to come here this morning?

Where are you headed
with your red rucksack and crushed smile?

West of Eden

Returning to northern California, we find
the main north-south route closed by rockslides
so drive east over the Coast Range, up Interstate 5,
then back west over the mountains again, but
have to dodge falling rocks, high above the Trinity River

at a site where workers are repairing the road
after earlier slides. Arriving back at our rented house
we find the town's iconic lighthouse under threat as
the cliff thinks of letting go. And my favourite hiking path
has been blocked off as it crumbles to the sea. Rockslides,

mudslides, hillslides that take redbud, bright orange
California poppies, bare ledge and paradise with them,
everything slowly and inevitably, or all at once.
I walk the detour, follow a trail that enters a sort of tunnel
of overhanging evergreens, a place that reminds me

of *the banqueting hall and the sparrow.* I always thought
that image came from Chaucer, but recently I learned it's
older than that, part of an 8th century parable
by the Venerable Bede. The sparrow flies
from a wintry storm into a mead hall where everyone

is feasting, then soars out the far door, back into snow
and darkness, and its length of time in the light is like
this life we share. I had the wrong author, but today,
emerging from the green hall, I stand at the edge,
far from where I thought I wanted to live, and grateful.

Triptych at the Rim of a Hill

I

Once, when we lived on Cape Clear Island,
    I made a promise to myself

I've failed to keep: the sky was so bright
    that we'd taken a night walk

up the green road to the abandoned lighthouse,
    and I swore I would never again

live anywhere where I couldn't see the stars.
    Some island nights

we'd know the time by watching the Pleiades
    cross the skylight above our bed.

Sidereal time: time as measured by stars.
    I'm thinking of Cape Clear tonight

in Amsterdam, while reading Van Gogh's letters.
  When I have a terrible

need of – shall I say the word – religion,
    then I go out and paint the stars.

~

Large enough that I thought at first they were parrots,
    five wild parakeets

in the garden of our holiday rental. Wings
    the essence of green.

Thinking about bright colours as we walked
    to the Rijksmuseum,

but the first work that really struck me was a dark one –
dusky reds, somber blues, haloes of gold –

a 1435 oil painting from the Meuse Valley, *Scenes*
from the Life of Christ,

where the sun never appears in eighteen panels.
The Annunciation, the Nativity,

the betrayal in the garden, the Resurrection –
all the important things

happen under stars as big as Van Gogh's.
Constellations come right down

to shine on the whips of Pilate's soldiers. Even
the Crucifixion made midday stars bloom.

~

Dreamt we were entering a large park at night
but had to deposit

everything we were carrying – car keys, passports,
notebook, birth certificates –

in the free lockers near the entrance gate.
Later, we had to give up

even the keys to our lockers. It felt safe, but also
like death,

when those things that once defined us
will no longer be relevant.

We walked beneath the stars, heading
    for the rim of the hill and the far gate

that led to paradise. As if all important things
    happen under stars.

~

Walking back to our Airbnb after dark
    from the Van Gogh Museum,

stars so bright we think they should be reflected
    in the canals.

And I'm caught in an argument from
    over a century ago –

When Gauguin saw the series of sunflowers Van Gogh
    painted to greet him,

he said, *Shit, shit, everything is yellow: I don't even know*
    what painting is anymore.

So began the Colour Wars that raged
    even after Gauguin fled.

Yellow, too, were Van Gogh's constellations,
    those sunflowers of the night:

dark skies with paint so thick the canvases
    took a month to dry

even in the South of France. Blazing whirls
  above everything important.

The garden of the asylum in Saint-Rémy.
    The flaming cypress

and the starlit church. Even the giving up
    of keys.

~

Gauguin urged Van Gogh to adopt the Gospel
    of the Unreal. To paint indoors,

from memory. To work from the head
    instead of the eyes.

To serve the pure imagination.
    Van Gogh tried

for a few days, but then stepped outside
    to the banks of the Rhône,

striving to record the chance pleasures
  of the moment.

~

The canal waters run fast enough that stars
    can't be seen on the surface,

but they are up there nonetheless,
    burning, and I'd be lost

if I had to tell time by them.
    Wild parakeets

dream in the trees, larger than we would
    have thought,

the essence of green, but what does that matter
    when night has taken

all colour to itself. All around us, water moving
    and fish down there,

I can suddenly hear them, I hadn't thought
    anything lived in those canals

and now they glide by, unseen, swimming
    towards the North Sea.

II

Waking far from home, in night's thin regions,
    thinking there really might

be a paradise, but it is found chiefly
    in art, in certain books,

canvases or compositions that lift us temporarily
    into the transcendent.

I'd dreamt of a poet who arrived at his reading
    without his new work

so he asked me to retrieve it. His house was close by,
    near the sea, reached

by a series of footbridges. I gathered loose papers
    (somehow now it was Elizabeth Bishop

who waited for me at the library) and felt ecstatic
    to be in her house, surrounded

by her watercolours and manuscripts, then found
    a handwritten poem called 'Heaven on Earth'.

~

Even as a child, I found it hard to believe
    in an afterlife

and surely that influences my reading of Bishop's
    'The End of March'

as being an unbeliever's dream of heaven: *Perfect –*
but impossible! And I know

not to look for any paradise in this world: even if found,
expulsion's surely

inevitable. Still, I've long been tempted:
when I was nineteen,

I followed Thoreau's advice and sauntered,
not hiked around Ireland

(Thoreau says all true saunterers are seeking
the Holy Land).

I must have given locals something to smile at: a boy
who thought he was catching

glimpses of another world on small rainy roads
in Donegal.

And almost half a century later, haven't I just booked
tickets to travel to Finistère to visit

the small village where Paul Gauguin and Meijer de Haan
once unpacked with such excitement.

~

Before going back to sleep, I find the essay I've been
looking for, Adam Zagajewski's

treatise on *otium*, the Latin word for *a serene, aimless*
unhurried meditation,

and yes, here it is, *otium* is *a paradise of literature,*
a *cozy infinity* of reading.

But one of my oldest friends died recently,
a daily communicant

who made the next world seem almost possible, and if she
read these thoughts

about art as paradise, I can just hear the mirthful, throaty
hoot she would have offered.

~

And isn't there something monstrous
about the paradise of art,

given the misery of the girl I once cared for
on the children's unit,

raped and tortured to the point that I couldn't
imagine a future for her.

Or the family ripped apart when a mother
is sent back to Mexico

after living twenty-one years
in the Promised Land.

Yes, granted, every artist is a monster.
But some of them at least

are searching. Zagajewski calls the goal *a certain*
ungraspable 'something',

or *a radiant 'something'*. Radiant, yes
    and sometimes rent.

Like the unknowable registers that Mexican mother
        explored,

singing and humming in the back of the bus, recording
        messages for her children.

III

Marie Henry, recently returned from Paris
with an infant daughter

and no husband, must have found conservative Brittany
a strange place for Gauguin

to be searching for paradise when he arrived at her inn.
And when the Dutchman de Haan

showed up two weeks later, he seemed to Marie
to be another eager but naïve seeker.

Meijer de Haan was short and hunchbacked,
but he was a scholar, excited

by his painting, and he made her laugh. Two artists
(there would be more, soon)

and their black-haired innkeeper humming to herself
in the kitchen.

Marie couldn't accept that Gauguin was someone
historic enough (his words)

to justify abandoning his wife and children,
but she thought she could tell

what sort of man Meijer was from the painting
he did of her breastfeeding Mimi.

She'd never felt so seen. He caught the moment
when the eyes of both

mother and child are half-closed and the world
    is one benign flow.

Having traded in his dark palette for Gauguin's
    brighter colours, he was

a man on the verge of a breakthrough. True,
    when he came to Le Pouldu,

he was in the early stages of the consumption
    that would kill him,

but he seemed to be able to gaze from afar
    at the Promised Land,

to begin painting bright landscapes of it, and for Marie
    and Mimi and himself

he would try to make a home in those warm colours
    (he actually said that).

~

Money was scarce, so the painters
    bartered with Marie,

decorating the walls of her dining room.
    Meijer began

with Breton women scutching flax; Gauguin
    contributed a self-portrait

with both halo and snake; Meijer painted
    a still life with Mimi

reaching out for a piece of bright fruit and, though
it was the sort of painting

when one isn't sure what sort of fruit
that shape might be,

her delight and desire are clear, and Meijer said
he'd like never again to paint a still life

without a child in it, holding her hands out
as if it were really possible to seize

that which we long for, that shimmering something;
then Gauguin added a girl at her spinning

as boats with red sails passed and an angel appeared
with mauve wings and undulating sword.

~

They were at best an unruly household, the painters
barefoot, sometimes shirtless.

But for a time, Marie Henry's inn by the sea became
a place of painting, music and play.

And if, by year's end, the paradise that had glimmered
in Brittany seemed elsewhere –

Meijer would have followed Gauguin to Tahiti
if health and money had allowed –

hadn't they achieved something, hadn't it been worth it?
Ask Marie, who cooked and cleaned for them

and was pregnant with Ida by the time Meijer set off
for Holland, leaving a large

Hebrew Bible and his paintings, including the one
of her nursing her daughter. And the still life

with Mimi reaching towards that one bright piece of fruit
that defies identification –

an apple or tomato or something else? It is red.
It is almost pulsating.

~

Who told Marie of Meijer's death? His family
wouldn't have written;

hadn't his father called her *a less*
than nothing?

Even though she was carrying the old man's grandchild.
Or, because she was.

Since Meijer died in Amsterdam, perhaps
Johanna van Gogh,

the widow of his friend, sent word? It would have been
five years since Meijer left,

and maybe – knowing how complicated
matters had been –

Madame van Gogh thought the news might
simplify things. Or was his absence

already a sort of death, dark flames
    that fed

on their own ashes until there was a certain luminous
    emptiness

where life could start again for her, this time with a writer
    in a new home up the coast?

~

Meijer's paintings adorned her new walls like bright birds
    that fly back and forth

between past and present. For that, Marie
    might have been grateful.

For the rest, well, he left her carrying
    her second child.

I imagine her hearing of his death and feeling less grief
    than she expected.

Then next morning, setting bulbs in the garden,
    perhaps she howled for Meijer de Haan.

Sometimes, we don't let ourselves
    hear the news at first.

~

Marie moved to Kerfany-les-Pins with her *keepsakes*
    of nirvana: the paintings

Meijer left behind instead of rent, or himself;
work Gauguin later returned to claim

though the judge ruled against him – the artist was beaten
by sailors when he kept harassing her;

and the little sketch of a bridge that van Gogh made
that Meijer collected.

Would Vincent have joined them at Marie's inn?
He wrote from the asylum in Saint-Rémy,

exploring that possibility, and it is tempting to dream up
a different ending for him,

supported by a wider community of artists,
healed by long walks

and painting by the sea. But Gauguin advised against it
and, as the Breton idyll

was becoming a shambles, it's hard to think
the scene change would have saved Vincent.

~

Paradise was Gauguin's word, not van Gogh's –
a friend or a few like minds

stretched the limits of what Vincent could hope for.
And seven years after the bullet

entered van Gogh's stomach, Gauguin tried to overdose
on arsenic, having completed his masterpiece,

*Where Do We Come From? What Are We? Where Are We
Going?* During his Eden experiment in Tahiti,

he suffered from heart disease and syphilis,
and his favourite daughter

died in Denmark. Day by day the wound grew deeper –
unable to do anything for her,

what use is painting when we can't save
those we love?

He recovered from the poison and produced
more dreams of the tropics,

but it was over, he knew that, he
turned to the wall

and glared at it, refusing to speak to those
who offered comfort.

~

Meijer de Haan eagerly experimented with the torque
Gauguin gave to colour,

but structurally he held off, wanting to honour
the things around him.

He told Marie that what he was trying to paint in *Maternity*
was both this world and a vision,

and she said, *It got very cold, waiting for you
to have that vision.*

~

Meijer traded his share in the family business
for the chance to paint, so it's easy

to blame his relations for withholding his allowance,
forcing an end to what they called his *dalliance*

with Marie Henry, but tonight, reading how the family—
brothers, children, grandchildren—perished

decades later in the camps with three-quarters
of Holland's Jews,

fault feels irrelevant. As if the angel with the sword
guards even the gates of the everyday.

~

There were moments in Le Pouldu when life seemed
elevated and after Marie moved to Kerfany,

hoping for a more sustainable happiness, I like to imagine
she sometimes felt she was inside

that glowing realm again, with her children
or in her garden,

as if heaven was a movable celebration, everywhere
if one could see it. But if she

had tried to paint it, I suspect her paradise would have
been nothing like Gauguin's tropics.

Maybe she would have tried to capture a moment
    returning from her morning's walk,

everything somehow strange and wonderful, the blue
    of the sea at the end of the road,

Ida and Mimi playing in the garden, a flock of curlews
    rising and calling

and all of it happening at once – she opens the gate
    and there are the children,

the sunflowers, the gusting south wind, the clamour
    of ascending birds.

About the Author

Theodore Deppe is the author of *Children of the Air* and *The Wanderer King* (Alice James Books, 1990 and 1996); *Cape Clear: New and Selected Poems* (Salmon, 2002); *Orpheus on the Red Line* (Tupelo, 2009); and *Beautiful Wheel* and *Liminal Blue* (Arlen House, 2014 and 2016).

He holds a Master of Fine Arts degree from Vermont College. A recipient of two grants from the National Endowment for the Arts and a Pushcart Prize, he has been writer-in-residence at the James Merrill House in Stonington, Connecticut, and Phillips Academy in Andover, Massachusetts.

Ted has taught creative writing in graduate programmes in the US, Ireland and England. He is on the faculty of the Stonecoast Master in Fine Arts programme, and he directs Stonecoast in Ireland, which brings graduate students from the University of Southern Maine to study in Ireland.

He worked as a registered nurse for twenty years while teaching poetry and fiction classes. Since 2000, he and his wife, poet Annie Deppe, have, for the most part, made their home on the west coast of Ireland. They presently live in Connemara. They are dual citizens of the US and Ireland.